To:

_____

From:

_____

Note:

_____
_____
_____
_____
_____

Mating Habits

Couples Guide

a-z

Joanne de Simone

Drawings by
S. L. Heiden

Moonlight Garden
Publications

Cover art and drawings by S.L. Heiden.

ISBN: 978-1-938281-22-8
Paperback Large Print Edition

Library of Congress Control Number: 2023932701

Published 2023, Moonlight Garden Publications, an imprint of Gazebo Gardens Publishing, LLC., Renton, WA.
www.GazeboGardensPublishing.com

Printed in the United States of Amerca.

An A-Z guide
to letting
better instincts
defeat
baser impulses.

"Man is the
only animal that blushes
—or needs to."

Mark Twain

Allow for slips and stumbles along the way.

Build emotional boundaries made of balloons.

Cheer each other on even amid calamities.

Dance barefoot together in daybreak's dew.

Encourage each other to expect miracles.

Free yourselves to find self-fulfillment.

Grant
each other
the gift
of
generosity.

Hold hands wherever you happen to be.

Ignite insights from apparent illusions.

Just stop and do a jaunty jig together.

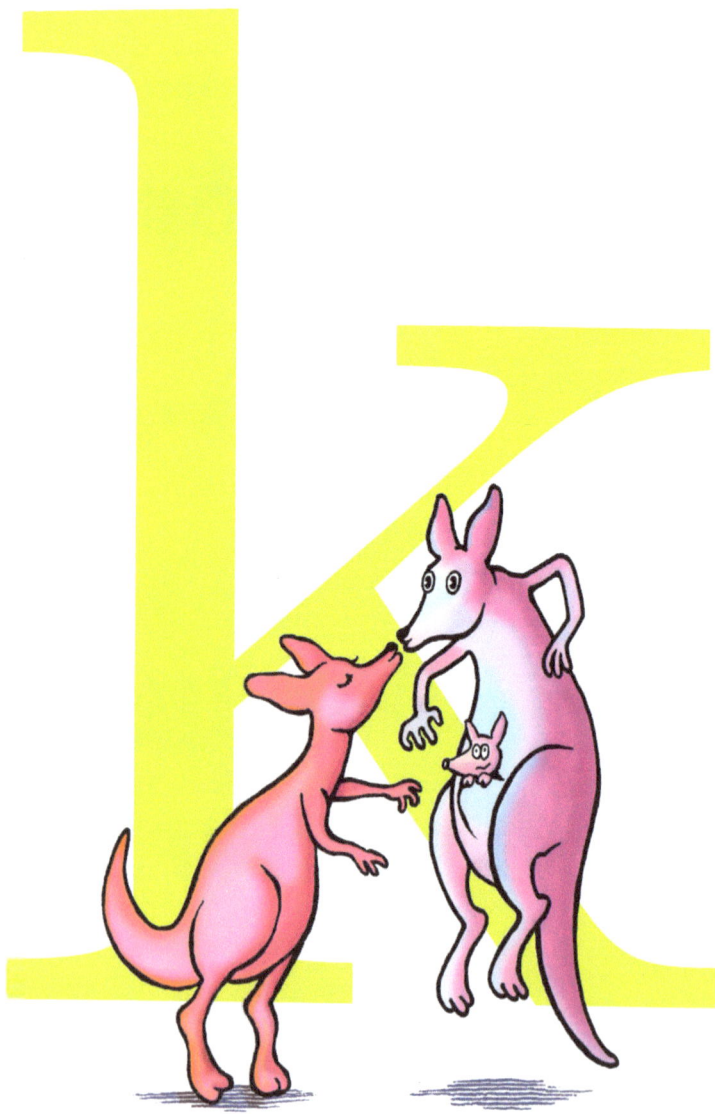

Kickstart kinetic energy with kisses.

Linger longer after love-making.

m

Make hay
in
a
classic
Model A.

Now
and then
sit a spell
with
nature.

Open
your minds
to opt
for new
adventures.

Pass
a note
of praise
on a paper
napkin.

Quell quarrels with quiet questions.

Revisit the reasons for your mutual attraction.

Sit

together

in silence

and stare

at the stars.

Take
the time
to talk about
something
trivial.

Upset
the
apple cart
and
juice it up.

Voice your vexations sotto voce.

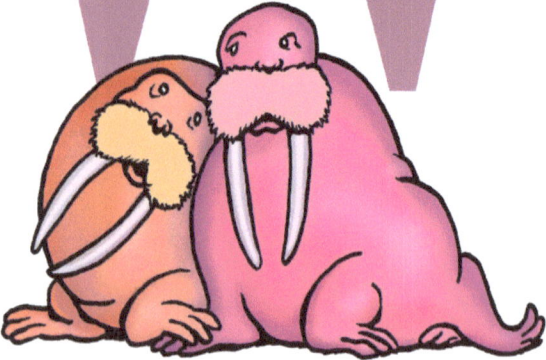

Wish
each other
wonders
with
words.

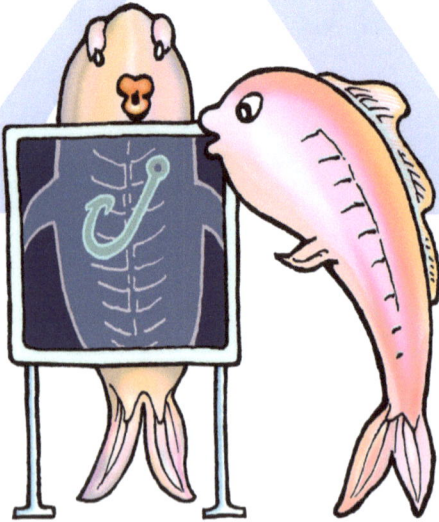

X-ray and expel irrational baggage.

Yearn for each other and learn from each other.

Zap zone outs with high-kicking zeal.

Author Joanne de Simmone

Writer, award winning playwright, poet, and film historian, Joanne's books include "The Metro Cats, Life in the Core of the Big Apple" and "The Peculiar Plight of Milicent Wryght," both set in Manhattan. She also penned "Songs from Under the El, Memories of Life in the Dark," her personal story of growing up in Brooklyn, NY. She held a BA in Film, Literature, and Creative Writing and lived on the east end of Long Island, NY. Joanne passed away in May 2022.

Illustrator S. L. Heiden

S. L. Heiden lives in NYC and is unshakeable in the conviction that cartoons are the best explanation.

The a to z critters: aardvark, bear, cat, duck, elephant, fox, giraffe, hedgehog, iguana, jaguar, kangaroo, lion, mouse, newt, owl, penguin, quetzal, rhinoceros, squirrel, T-rex, unicorn, vicuna, walrus, x-ray fish, yak, and zebra—in case you were wondering.

www.ingramcontent.com/pod-product-compliance
Lightning Source LLC
Chambersburg PA
CBHW041354270326
41934CB00029BA/5